·The·

BLUESTONE
WALK

Also by Edward Nobles

Through One Tear

· The ·
BLUESTONE
WALK

—POEMS

EDWARD NOBLES

A KAREN & MICHAEL BRAZILLER BOOK

PERSEA BOOKS / NEW YORK

For their faith in my work over distance and time—Michael Braziller, Richard Burgin, Marjorie Perloff, and Donald Revell—my gratitude.

Grateful acknowledgment is made to the editors of the following magazines for publishing these poems, some in earlier manifestations: *Boulevard*, "The Bluestone Walk," "Astronomy," "History," "Vogue"; *Colorado Review*, "Love Itself"; *Columbia Review*, "Longing"; *Commonweal*, "Heart Ear"; *Denver Quarterly*, "Antiques," "Field & Stream"; *Gettysburg Review*, "American Home"; *Kenyon Review*, "Fissure," "Through a Drop of Rain"; *Long Shot*, "The Grand Canyon"; *Mississippi Review*, "The Green Bottle"; *New Orleans Review*, "Fortune"; *Quarterly West*, "The Etched Catastrophe"; *Tar River Poetry*, "The Values of Stone"; *William and Mary Review*, "Contention"; *Witness*, "Cleansing: A Saga," "Once Again, It's Over"; *Yellow Silk*, "Transmigrations of the Innocents." "Heart Ear" also appeared in the anthology *Staring Back: The Disability Experience from the Inside Out*, edited by Kenny Fries (Penguin USA, 1997).

Persea Books, Inc.
171 Madison Avenue
New York, New York 10016

Library of Congress Cataloging-in-Publication Data

Nobles, Edward.
    The bluestone walk : poems / Edward Nobles.
        p. cm.
    "A Karen & Michael Braziller book."
    ISBN 0-89255-247-6 (alk. paper)
        I. Title.
PS3564.O27 B58 2000
811'.54—dc 21   00-028482

Designed by Rita Lascaro
Typeset in Minion

Manufactured in the United States of America
First Edition

for Kelly

&

for Lydia and Hadley, my daughters

And in memory of my mother, Jean Hartley Rae Nobles

CONTENTS

I. THE BLUESTONE WALK

II. TWELVE MAGAZINES

III. For All Time

IV. A Small Cluster of Stars

· I ·

THE BLUESTONE
WALK

The Bluestone Walk

I barrow the dust through pine.
The best-pulverized drifts—too light
even for earth, even if stone—over
the four-by-forty-foot trench,
and, wind's whim,
sifts back into my tracks,
the hours, my mind. It traces
the leaves, the lumber, the sky,
bequesting a majestic purplish hue
to this third work day, a gray
March day, gray since before
spring started, just a few days ago.

I knew, when I had started, this job
wouldn't end. They never end
exactly right, in pace with what's wanted,
when each step is so carefully
plotted against a new start. The next
job can wait; others can bide my time.
I level the line, pad my knees,
and start stone. Four hours later,

the dust takes on life,
acquires design: squares and rectangles,
rectangles and squares—four sets
of four set dimensions, each stone
hammered, wrestled, jostled,
forced within the four-
foot width. The wind
drives west while the stone
moves north. No one is here
and the wind-weathered cracks

dance a neat pattern, forty feet from the house,
over which I, now a small boy,

leap, avoiding the dark.
A widow's wax,
the streets are asphalt, laid by machines.
A school hour, too young for school,
my blue sneakers dangling,
I hug the wooden box to my chest,
and look inside.
Choices.

I take the small bird, traced
with dust, and prod
it loose, spirit toward pine.
Cheeks against stone, I finger my name
carved deeply into the gray
of this handpainted cage. This spring
runs level with death, the underside
of dust, a bluestone walk—too light
even for earth, even if stone—a four-
by-forty-foot path that leads,
from here to childhood
and back, one slow stone step

across time.

Heart Ear

To half hear
is to be without direction. Everything
moves toward you from the right.
Even a lover's kiss, on the earlobe of the
left, is felt, but slightly; the alluring breath
streams around the head and enters at
the other end of night: a spirit's touch
against the window. It flutters there, in the rain,
intent on entry, but it cannot knock.

Is it the mystery, or the mistrust,
that the left ear fails to hear?

A child of five, fevered with measles, my heart ear bled
and bottled-up with wax. The pain was fierce
and good for nothing but my mother's worried eye
which was worth a lot
in a house of seven peers. One night, the ear's shrieking
burnt a hole into the sheet. Or so it seemed, as I held my head
against the pillow and cringed inward; the aching entered
and endured.

Dead now, it treasures more
the subtle world of night. Sometimes
the good ear's insight is so perfect
I can't bear my present life. It is then
the past crawls
all the way around the rim
of years, to tap lightly, like a spider,
against the senseless drum.

Sentences

The sledgehammer cracks
like my father's heavy shouts
until the stone starts to break.
The sound then is different.
Only a thumb's touch is needed.

The division is final.

Fissure

The light, broken by a branch,
collapses through the barn, one side
to the other. One pine falters, then spreads
its wings against the wood—both forms
miraculously planed
into a carpenter's vision,
rotted and gray. Finality
on the road; no one dare stop it.
My father draws near, dimming the light.
Winter. How then to enter
this haven of gray, this heaven
of age-split wood?

Two crows up-pull, sockets specked
with my reflection. I look over the rims
of the blood-shot dark. To the right,
a fallen sun. To the left,
the dark trees rising. Half of me drops
to the half-hot flesh. The other half
scours a tree. Vertigo impends.
My mother cries from beneath the earth.
Her fragile heart shakes, a first-burst seed.
Every year, memory blossoms. And every year,
the leaves descend, trailing
a death path round the world.
Desire follows, clothed in black wings.

Through a Drop of Rain

I saw the crow
through a drop
of rain, my face
pressed toward it
against the glass.
Its perfect
shape
rocked up and
down
in its need.

In my soul,
I pushed it off
onto one
wing and then
the other. It flew
determined
into the dark
and perched
on the topmost
branch.

Its heart-eye scanned
the known
and the unknown.

In reality
it remained
below, there

in the rain-
soaked grass,
pecking,
approaching,
hesitantly
my parked car.
But I

didn't stick around.
I was there
above, beyond,
still intent, still
scanning
the dark.
I placed
my hunger
high
above my need.

A Pattern of Wealth

…and with ambitious aim
Against the throne and monarchy of God,
Raised impious war in Heaven and battle proud,
With vain attempt.
                    —Milton, *Paradise Lost*

The hard, well-seasoned oak
burns clean, driving the near-
invisible smoke
straight up the flue
and clear on into
a snow-white sky—
in my imagination,
I see the perfect
fire, encased with the perfect
stone, granite or field, with the back

dramatically sloped
and charred, the shot sparks rising,
perfectly, in sublime transcendence,
when I toss a test
to the flames, an old nail.

But the grate is empty; no one is home.
No romantic, rustic warm scene
burns off the chill, a cold
that doesn't exist in this controlled
central world. I pry
the burnt brick facing from the wall
to unhouse the past. The dried mortar
crumbles, opening a gash
at the side of the flue
the size of a man. I lean in, holding the wall,

to wire the back. Something must hold
the mortar that holds the stone
beside the stones' own weight—only the beams,
these sheets of wire, and the staggered
strips of steel. I cart the bricks

and stack them in the yard. I am shifting
the history of brick to the elegance
of marble—rich, royal, machine-cut marble
with stunning dark grains that lavishly
swirl through the blue, a pattern of wealth.
I lay the large tiles in an outline on the rug.
This polish is beyond me, an aspiration—
five-foot sides
topped with an eight-foot god: the mantle.
Is it the burn of fear or joy

I feel when, still pounding outward
at a tough last brick,
I slip a stroke and drive my sledge
against the throne and solid monarchy
of marble?

The Green Bottle

We adventured along the beach,
picking up horseshoe crabs, cracking the shells,
rotating the rotted seaweed up over our heads, lashing it down
against each other, kicking the discarded castles,
the skeletal debris of a tireless ocean.

The beach was empty, private,
somewhere up along the Atlantic.
Three or four acres past
that snow-sprinkled dune, the owner's mansion
conspired against us—angry eyes—
but I was thinking of something else. Or, rather,
someone else.

Then you found an old discarded bottle.
This one had no note, but you yelled for me
to join you anyway.
I saw you in a blur as I approached.
The bottle was beautiful, green, a worn swirled green.
You couldn't see through the glass; you could only see
the glass. It was lovely.
I fondled the bottle until my fingers

lost themselves in the touch. I placed the top to my lips,
tongued its roundness, its cool polished silk.
The beach and all the Atlantic
sounded around me,
lonely to my touch.

To Be Together

The ducks roam the pond's embankment,
two or three together, rarely alone.
They love the warm drizzle that blurs the lights.
Toward them, the house windows
set out their typical lure
of a different kind of light, the warmth
and happiness, a gunshot
hidden from within, moving forward with precision.

I take my chances, straying onto the lawns,
hoping to catch a glimpse of some final gesture.
But I see only what is there: a half-rolled shade,
a table with two empty plates, an elbow.
Even when the shades are drawn, the inside
moves outward into the night. Pulling
or pushing from behind, it's you

that keeps me here. I see your eyes
staring up at me
from the raindrops,
in the puddles, in the mud. Or I'd like to see them there
with my hands in an oily ringlet around your throat.
At least then there'd be something. You
down there, out here, with me,
patiently together in the rain.

Contention

The base stones toe a rugged line.
Moss-stained and spud-round
from eruptions of weather, the upper
rows hold, steadied by chinks,
a dignified mass. Four ton of stone
contracts to four feet of wall.
Start at the pine, move north,
up-grade, there, to the narrow ones,
bark-stripped and dead.

My heartbeat rises and leans
its heavy jaw against my rib;
knocks bone and builds. I shrug it off
and lift another stone. Nothing
can break my will. The sledge hammer
shatters and bites
off perfect chunks to fill
all space. No light! No light!
The light that can be seen,
that should be seen, will be seen,
and gapped with stone. I knock
space off to fill space in.

The gray night, green-tinged,
cracks against this earth.
I'll work all night, beyond
it, if it takes, beyond time.
Each thing lifts, hauls,
and rolls directly into place.
My muscles ache; my spirit, walled,
still loves. Love, with all
its waste, stacks
its labor against my work.

At the Sanctuary

We who hear you, hear you.
Sound from the thicket,
lush with night.
I sit down on a fat log,
still wet with rain,
half-lodged in the marsh mud,
and listen. No sound. Just hearing.

Spread out, my hands soak up
the log's textured slime. My fingertips
pulsate, breathing.

Then a small shrub, rattled
by the wind, lets its cupped
rain pools fall
against my ear. I look up

to the tree line that tugs to the east
toward you. And then the bus
pulls toward me, at me, its huge tires scraping
the granite curb, the wet silver sides
burning in the streetlights.

I step aside and notice
everyone has raincoats, everyone
looks the same. At first,
you look the same. Then,
the difference. Something in the way your left brow
pulls down against the curbstone
of my seeing. *Hear you.*
"Move aside man, move aside! I'll miss my bus!"
Not even curses; I hear nothing.

You pull me toward you (a courtesy to strangers).
You tell me there, then, now,
with the silver bus still in sight, three blocks down,
stopped at the next street light, at the church. The blind
disembark.

Remember how we stood
in the silent stone arches
of a different church, for so many hours,
one clear hot summer day, years ago, its squat steeple
reflected in the Hancock's blue glass, avoiding
nothing (no rain), holding each other,
not praying, not needing.
We hear you.

Someone knocks—a revelation?—elbows
their way to the curb. WALK. Time. Now or
never, they cross. I lower my voice *(Hear you?)*. Pride—
your raincoat turning—is a shield, as everyone knows.

The marsh sounds emerge, louder, louder.
Then, the echoing reconnaissance of rain.
Then: you. Again: you.
Then the engines, the black spinning,
total deafness, shrapnel, early childhood,
alcohol, my mother's death.

Lakeside

Sometimes the wind
wins out and waves
carry light
in the form of knives.
Then it is blade against blade,
steel against steel
and glorious sparks.
And a loon floats by, slowly,
almost as if a still life,
excruciatingly slow,
like the wait for love,
a mother's or a father's,
their painful lives long over,
and it keeps to itself
its echoed black ring,
its distinctive cry, its laughter.

The Values of Stones

1.

These chinks between the stone,
how often we ignore them,
the way the moments are forgotten
when one counts a life with years.

2.

A large ugly stone and
no face worthy
but outward chipped
with a quick downward sledge
and you have a pile of difference,

a perfect fit
for each and every hole.

3.

The beauty of a stone
is intrinsic. Unlike a brick
which is burnt, near-perfect,
from a mold.

4.

When the wall's complete
there's always stone to spare.
You work with them, sizing each,
building with great difficulty
in your mind
as you toss them in the ditch.

5.
A walk through the woods and there
you see it: the exact right stone!

But that wall was finished
(the house, where was it?)
several years ago.

6.
Memory leaves the wall;
and death
of memory, nothing but one
stone.

Child on a Raft

Each day finds me
a child on a raft
in the small swamp
behind our house.
The rotted gray boards
are a source of pride.
I nail them to themselves
and create a reason
to float.

          Half sinking—
it wants to sink—
I push first in one
direction, to the dead oak
with its great roots
as rotted as my raft,
and then I turn
in another direction
toward my favorite side,
furthest from the house.

There, a welcoming bend
hides me from myself
and the small stand of trees
looms all around me
in the slight dark.
It is wonderful.

But, always, there is an end
to the feelings, an end
to each shore's treasure.

Why can't I always stay afloat,
forever, just stand still,
lightly rotate
in the ripples, here in the middle?
Why can't I hold onto
this tuft of weeds
and never go back
or in any direction, toward
any shore?

I go back.
First in one direction, and then
the other, back and forth
across the hours. Movement
must be the reason
for the day. And the night?
The night finds me here too,
in dreams
amidst the water, the wet weeds,
the dead oak with its night roots
as rotted as the day's. Only now,

everything is distant, hidden
in time's mystery, a deep happiness
that floats with me, within me,
on my small raft.

· II ·

Twelve
Magazines

Fortune

This silver brooch is beautiful: spider-fine
filigree, bordered by two bands and then a row
of circles, each its own creature, a coin-like design,
all tarnished, slightly dented, and twisted in a bow.
Unclasped from the pin, I unstick it from her sweater.
Some things are meant to come undone. But why
must everything appear in terms of money? Even this
seat, in which I stab the brooch, I had to buy,
smothered in smoke, from a bunch of brokers trying to better
one another, against a lover, for what they'd probably never miss.

But the hard-bought chair is beautiful, too. All rosewood,
except the cushion, which is an intricate scene
done in point, of a lion and his mate in somber pose. Should I
choose to die, theirs would be the place I'd mean
when I whispered for taut black trees and claw-torn deer
stitched in blue. And now one stag wears a bow.
I love the way the silver pin
slid so smoothly from the cashmere swell, and how I know
where the bow had been, and what forces steer
the fingers and the heart. That lions sin

is clearly in their eyes. There's no doubt
this craftsman knew his task. Look at the back,
how the leaflets rise, but how the two flowers sweep downward in long
    pout.
Or how the wood so perfectly swerves to catch the light or its lack.
Even the arms, on which drunken vines weave, were done
to perfection. Yet who was this carver? Did he create for one who
    loved as Lear,
lingering long hours in the dark, dreaming of what sword to strike

the head off of a daughter? I unpluck the brooch and pull it near
to run along my face. The blackish silver has the features of a nun.
No faith can buy the tiny coins, the creatures in a spin, the web-like

tracery weaving in every fraction of an inch.
I take the seat and set the brooch down on my lap.
I touch the pin and feel each flower pinch
into my back, and wonder how evening wraps
the hours, the decades, the seconds with a bow. Quietness
exerts its influence on both the lion and the vine.
Rosewood in every wood and from the blue the deer
leap into nonexistence for those who love to dine
in dark interiors, where black trees range the skies and skies express
the furniture, the magazines, the clothes removed. With love and fear.

American Home

Chippendale, American,
with curved aborted leaf
and reeded spool, circa 1802,
this bridal bed, though pine,
retains its mahogany
reddish hue, a result
of thickened ox blood
and fresh New England cream.

The high heels, hushed
from their seductive click,
look innocent, unable to lure
with motion or the meaningful
turn.
                I watched them fall,
each one alone, with seeming
intent, over the edge
of this tall
                and vacant bed.

Threads

To fall by the weight
of movement, desire,
or the distracted touch?
The protracted
possibility, the unsettling
hope, the slide of silk
along itself, red
against red, the dull
and the shimmer.
Spread loose, fall fully,
come undone.
What have you? Voyeur?
When no one is here?
I watch. I roll the ribbon
out, tongue-like
along the rug, a ten-foot runner
that takes me down
the hall and into
a darker room. I wait.
The thin silk
measures less than a yard.
Seven feet left for all else: a body
pierced with arms. This pattern
takes me places
I never meant to go. I follow it
backward, red, twisted in a bow,
through the room and
up and down this hall.
I hold the bottom
of my shoe, lean back
against the wall, and watch

as the thread moves back
through the heddles
of the loom, to the mulberry
and the worm.

Astronomy

Austerely, shrouded in their distance,
lumbering in silence, the planets move
across the wrinkled page. Another instance
of when the unseen can't fail to soothe
by being betrayed. Somewhere—a private collection? the Louvre?—
in a back room, under dusty lights, I saw
a similar locket. It too had a single groove
of gold, a small etched telescope, and some astronomical law
I couldn't understand or even read. I draw

the locket off and hold it close
beneath the ceiling's light. The plaster has its own laws
of movement, its blank contrasts and frozen coast.
The swirled ridges mirror the planets on the wrinkled page.
The locket, on a tiny hinge, opens to another age:

Here, two ancient fish tear into water made of gold.
The marshy shore, around which they swim, is merely suggested, small
tufts of weed and a few swirls for sand. Above is a bold
full moon, and a couple faint clouds. I read somewhere that sometime
    in July all
nine planets line the evening sky. I can't recall
if this is every year, or only once or twice—perhaps never.
Around the rim roll what look like balls,
and yet are joined; so if not planets, a chain or signs of weather?
Whoever commissioned this locket had conviction and meant forever.

That's clear in every detail: the approaching fish, the clouds, the moon,
the planets and the golden earth, the way the two halves come together

with a tiny latch and lock, the enigmatic cover. The room
shines with nothing but what this artist saw in a strange dimension of
    light.
The ceiling's plaster, even in shadow, stays white.

Vogue

This mirror contains emotions of love
gone wrong, feelings that wrack
the heart, and wound the world. The frame
is brass, solid, but not
traditional in design: a six-foot, dove-
tailed rectangle, with the brass rolled back
in a bruised ripple of light:

> small brass waves
> falling, slow-motion,
> still-born,
> against the wall,
> then drained
> in its white.

The glass, I'm to blame,
is cracked. I hit it with my hand
when I drew the purse off, hauling
it greedily to my chest
and then turning. I can't understand
how it happened, but the mirror
copiously echoed its breaking
through the room. Nothing
happens now but the light. Just a second
and then the scene dissolves

before it reappears. At first,
I'm uncertain. Deadly snake or lizard skin?
The strap, a blackish sheen, is slick, and the snap
pops open with a fearful click. The body
bulges with what beauty will devour in its thirst.
The skin, dyed purple, is diced: a variety of thin
fluctuating squares. I lift the cover, a small
curved flap. Inside:

lipstick (red), Bonne Bell,
a tan compact, two
bottles of cheap
perfume, black gloves, a
brush and comb set, candy,
the cross, this scrap

of paper with a number and a name, a map,
marked, of a strange city, some unlabeled pills,
a magazine of fashion, crammed—
I don't know how—into this mid-sized reptile of a bag.
I open the magazine and place it on my lap.
I'd rather stare anywhere than into the broken glass.
The brass could no doubt use a shine. On the left-hand
page is a truly seductive teen. She's staring out to sea, holding on
tightly, to some iguana on her knee. To the right,
is the same beauty, this time coiled
together with a snake. I place

the purple purse
to my parched
lips and laugh
at the love-
lorn looks, the
reptiles, the re-
flected photographs.

World Art

You can see it there, hanging on the wall,
beside a reddened chef, dressed in white, full of fear,
it seems, because his pie is about to fall.
It's meant for the couple with famished hands that clasp
each other as if they themselves were the desired feast.
Anyway, beside this poster hangs a black brassiere

on a small brass hook. But though a black brassiere,
I love the defiled modesty of white. However, the papered wall
is predominantly white. And white against white is too subtle a feast.
I want the real classic: a line of black lace, a premonition of fear,
and then that something special: a lion-tight clasp
that wants to open and then close. Before it falls.

In the painting you can tell the season's fall.
It's like the aura of a beloved brassiere.
Dead leaves beneath the table, the desperate dogs that clasp
their teeth and arch their bones against the wall.
One old guest stares out the window with what looks like fear.
He sees the tree bent forward and two stray birds that feast

on nothing but the wind. Even the couple, with their large feast,
are shaken. Forever, the chef's pie is about to fall.
I slide the dark silk off with a tinge of fear.
There's nothing like the warmth of a black brassiere.
I hold it to my face, another wall.
The cups, the perfect contours, the silvered clasp.

For weeks or months, it seems, I clasp
it there, not knowing for sure the exactness of the feast.
I stare for hours at the wall,

the Brueghel and the blatant light. Leaves fall,
and, in the Metro, darken—a black brassiere.
Nothing can fill the darkness, though, not even the fear

couples feel when forced to part, a fear
the near-dead cherish and the coming winters clasp.
I sink into the night snow of the black brassiere
and wonder at the patterns on which I feast.
Of what passions did the painter dream? Do decades fall,
black on white, and move like death against the wall?

Catholic Digest

What is a room
without music,
a cast-iron urn,
a bowl of wax fruit?
A bronze lamp,
its flexible arm
pushed forward
for better light?
It stands
behind the bed,
shade fluted, one rib bent.
Motions for the missing
and what could have been.
One earring removed
was enough. I hold it up
in the light, a broken twig.

Field & Stream

1.

Half-hid behind thick
German glass, old glass
sensitively blurred
with delicate
scars and bubbles,
the English plates
lean barely safely back,
a fragile sea,
against the wood. On each
of five, eight shells lie cast
beneath two slick
enameled swirls,
raised waves that pass,
ceaselessly held, direct-
ly against no shore.
Adeptly, though, each
spiral shifts, transforms
itself, as if by fate,
into four blurred
branches with jagged
white leaves. Love's
genesis captures
this beauty that swells
behind glass, in memory
with fears
circling forever, outward
toward fields
and streams. It matters
when love creates
round this way in dreams.

2.

A hat encircles
the head. The head
gone, the hat exists.
I toss it, with questions,
to the light. It falls
upon itself, a black hole.
Inside, I find a tag: "Hat
by Hartley: New York."
Twisted right, the brim
proves red, more or less
horizontal, one side
pinned, by her, to the top, a hem-
isphere, but felt, so flat.
I want to fall, away
from this hat, off the edge
of my thoughts
into a field. (The numb
ones move intently
down streams.) I want
to hunt, no hat on my head,
through the mud, the swamp
water rising, my right
arm raised, the clear and
delicate
shudder, the shot. Something
stopped, then falling. I'm stuck
revolving in moments
of love, around the rim
of this room. Inside,
nothing. But a hat.

History

Arms spread, on the mantle sits some ancient god.
It's just the clock, but the way the body dips
so gently downward and then across, like lips
slowly parted after that long and fatal kiss, so odd,
it makes you think of a golden circle, or a lightning rod
that sparks along the hour. And toward evening the underworld slips
until time's all wrong, and the red camisole rips
against the minute hand. The fingers close; the ages nod.

History is held together by two rolled silk strings,
a little red lace, and a fortune of flames. On the clock
are painted numbers—Roman—and a name. On wings
one decade fades into another: frantic birds caught without a dock.
I stroke the body of this timepiece, emphatically, to see it ring,
but hear the rustled silk, and feel the ram-like hours lock.

Antiques

What burns more
than past, now fruitless, lust?

Restraint: a lingering waft
of her perfume
negates the present and dents
the mind. A coal box offers such
a promise of forgotten heat.
Archaic, it sits
here empty in our room, a useless relic,
purchased for its singularity,
its rustic charm: a burial raft
pushed forward through time,
from some Victorian city.

Under its colorful, witty
walnut lid of caterpillars carved
in a woolen spin, as if with a gardener's
inward hope
for spring, then summer's
coming heat, there's a rusted,
somewhat dented, metal bin.
(Note: the female moth lures
the male moth for miles
by virtue of what, inflamed,
she secretes.) Inside the tin's
coal black, there's a crack,
a nail-hole of light: the moon.

What will excite me, incense me,
sightless, back? Perfume.

Better Homes and Gardens

Chipped white ceramic,
with little green left,
legs knocked off,
hands clasped, upward dredged
distorted grimace,
a drunkard's image
of what a saint might be,

discovered late
one summer, a sole survivor,
precariously set
on top a metal pole,
before a kidney-shaped pool
filled to the rim with dirt,
one ladder leading down

into the dirt, bones, rocks,
dead algae, clothing, deflated
toys, inert chairs (no more floating),
corroded holders, lost drinks,
broken glasses, all things
someone felt worthy of burial,
easier than repair,

this frog, or is it toad?
eyes upraised, hands
frozen everlastingly in prayer
(Lord, take this body
and bend it back
into a womb-curl, let
the diminishing

bones crack
if they will),
sits in a corner on the floor;
I untie her green silk scarf
and offer back
a shroud of love,
its homely garden color.

Gourmet

The ivory flowers stand composed, locked
in a spurt of movement, a permanent dispersion
of petals. The pistils are black; as are the flames—leaves
that shoot upward, toward a red wooden sky. The darkening grain
sweeps the landscape, flocked
to the edges, urged on
by the curving of thin stems, the forced direction of gorged bees.
Every corner portrays the same scene, and each scene lies framed
by more inlay of spine, a delicate
design, from old Baroque keys
(played tuneless in wood).

Hair spilling, I think of Saxons
plundering the grassy moors of England.
The Norse left fragments with them in the thick
forests beside the church: symbols with their graves,
a font beside the stone. It seems wrong,
though, to destroy without a will to create, but I can
understand how some forcefully take when sick
with desire, that mad desperation to save
what is already lost. Forcefully taken, I grasp
this barrette—Celtic in design—and dream the past.

Square pegs in round holes (an odd quintet)
pin the lapped corners of this old
hope chest. Other than discarded keyboard flowers and small bees,
the box is plain: a redwood carcass with a large curved lid.
Melville must have met
one like it when he stole

across the continent, shipped out with drunken whalers across the sea.
Most seamen would be envious of such a find. They'd probably bid
                sarcastic remarks of false hate.
                Without love, what is there,
                    but the sea?

    Two emeralds in a setting of soft eighteen-karat
    gold, cloisonné enameled with bold
    black circles and red rectangles that hold
    the form together with a series of white lines.
    The pin is bone, sleek and pointed, knobbed at
    one end. I push it into the slot, which is folded
    back with the metal as it curves, so cold,
    against my ear, where I place it for a sign;
    I hear only the sea, and that church; two gravestones and a font.
    The circles spin; the emeralds and skeletal pin, frozen in
        motion, taunt.

    The lid opens and closes on long, straight
    hinges—steel with deep screws. Outside is nothing
but what we dream. And what, in moments half drowned, does any
    one dream
but the scars? sails that bellow outward, against insurmountable odds.
        And yet, perhaps too late,
        there's hope, mounting on wing
within an old wooden box: silver and gold, iron, steel,
towels and blue sheets, two pillows, a quilt, blankets bought
        (exposed and weak) on travels
        East or to the isles, lonely
          places never seen.

Night falling, the bruised world is filled
with a warped dimension, that dark melancholia embedded,
like love, into wood. Along with the chest, the other possessions
come alive. Even the room's empty light
has its own mind. Each and everything is willed
with desire and desire is the history of time. And yet did
one such as Melville (pictured in his room) fight against the darkness,
    or for its passions
that stunned him into art? On the next page is something more
    cheerful: white
flowers on porcelain cases. Then a variety of dishes, hand-painted,
    Taiwan;
an article on bone. Sometimes I want

        so badly, to lock this chest and sink
        in it down to the heartbone
        of the innermost sea. Instead,
        I close the lid and step outside,
        finally, into the wind, and flip
        the barrette, with all its beauty,

            into the naked sky.

· III ·

FOR
ALL TIME

Under Agreement

I want to live in the house next door
where no one touched a thing in years
except the lawn, which was cut
by small scissors, clump by clump,
by Mrs. Childs, the owner
who was born there. White hair bunned,
nightgown to heels, she'd lie stretched out
on the foot-long grass, sometimes in the night,
and cut it, snip by snip. It would take the entire summer
to not quite finish
the small front plot. And no help
from the neighbors wanted, but she'd talk.

And now she's dead and I want
her house, to lie on her bed and watch
the thick dust rise, the rain
dripping from the ceiling, its sound
loud and purposeful
through the broken panes.
I will sell my house and feed
deeply on decay, a dried
sea of sepia, while outside
the half-dead hemlocks will continue
undiminished. They will swallow
the house, the blackbirds, the sky.

And inside this world, the papered walls
will slowly collapse, and I will move
to the basement
with the dehydrated potatoes, and bolts,
and broken metal
toy soldier, which I'll march
back and forth

along the one clean line, the trench
I will make for him, shoveling
the heavy dust, mote by mote,
with the long curved nail
of my only remaining finger.

(And no one
will see me. And no one
to know.)

Oh, broken soldier, slow down.
I am tired
and my will to push hurts.

Cleansing: A Saga

The first apartment we lived in as a family,
a couple of blacks moved into the building.
This, as you may well guess,
completely destroyed our happiness.

Our next apartment was beautiful—nice high ceilings
and two large windows for the plants—
but a large Oriental family took over as landlords,
and so we left, taking every last leaf.

We moved East, but the growing population
of Puerto Ricans and Mexicans
sent us South, where we soon learned
a family of Jews
or Arabs bought the last house
on the block, ruining the neighborhood.

We had to move. We had no choice.
It was a hard life, and expensive, but we only did
what anyone else would do.
We had pride. We knew our place.

Finally, we centralized.
My wife and five children were so happy!
But, of course, nothing lasts forever.
A carload of whites unloaded,
and then more whites, and more, like rats,
and we were back on the road again.

Transients, we survived
as a family for several years. But then, my wife

left me, disgusted with my face. And the children
scattered, avoiding each other like the plague.

Here in the isolation ward,
everything is near from perfect.
There is a little plastic mirror on the wall.
I steer clear, circling it with raised fists.
Every day, I pull at my hair, bite myself,
and call myself names. Every night,

I knock my head against the wall,
spitting at my shadow, its alien tainted blood.

Love Itself

And I knew again what I'd known before—
That love itself is as false as air.
                    —Apollinaire

Love lingers at the tip of my tongue,
then a chair moves back
and she rises. The old seaside streets
create scribbles of madness
when seen from above. She lives there,
red hair down, ready for bed,
a new man waiting, with curly black hairs
on his chest, which is his head, he's all muscles, a god!

My hair is brown and straight, but waves
in salty sailor curls as I walk
eddying in the wind about the town.
My hands are tied in a permanent knot
behind my back. A red dog leads,
but lingers far away, like love,
and scatters into mercury if I approach.
My lover's left little pieces of distorting mirrors.
I try to join them together, but the shards
surface in different tongues: ten in Chinese,
twelve in Russian, two in Church Latin, and a slew
in the Languages of the Dead.

I ring the tiny bell of my best friend, André.
He's not home, or is home, but greets me
in an African mask, chatting in a cynical script.
I slump in his chair. The television blasts its usual colors,
reds and blacks. I watch and wonder:
where is she? It's late. They're probably in bed already,
his heavy hands marring her childlike breasts!

I jump up, hell fire, and storm
through the door, like a father. The moon
attacks me and the stars help out. I go down.
The prehistoric stone stars
twinkle upward as I fall. I make a wish.
I fall into sleep with all my clothes on.
They lie heavy, like scattered soldiers in a ditch.

Once Again, It's Over

You stare at yourself, no need for mirrors this time,
and that's all you do. The hat on the wall, held there by a nail,
holds your head. Its blue-white matches the pale blue of your hands.
The rain-swept wind leans against the door, beating it.

The door's screen, warped from wear, dissects her face
into a hundred squares. And when she turns,
she holds only anger, tears. Nothing to do now
but apologize, call up, drive over, bring candy.

But you turn to the sink and you see yourself.
You see yourself, and then you turn again.
When next you remember her, the peak moments,
it's too late to call. You close your eyes

knowing there's no one there at all—at the door,
in the rain, in the beaded black car
backing from the house. You stare,
and that's all you do, held there by a nail.

Transmigrations of the Innocent

1. *A monster then I may her mirrorise, since*
   she delights in such strange tragedies.

   If you could bend
   your head just right
   in the mirror, spotted
   from soap splashings, perfume,
   you would see her there
   on her back, the covers flown,
   the blue slip up over her breasts, pulled softly
   to the sides
   by their own weight. The fan

   rotates slowly from the bureau.
   Its circle, oscillated,
   distorts the image further,
   at the corner, through the window,
   if you could only see.

2. *Water, water, everywhere,*
   Nor any drop to drink.

   The walls are red. Small orange fish
   move like still lifes
   in the green ocean of their tank. If you were there,

   knees bent, hands on knees, looking through
   the water, plants, fish and glass,
   you would see her turn

to the side, one arm beneath
soft reaching flanks, her dark hair above
a black halo
circling, a little rippled and
blurred from where you bend.

3. *The essence of all science lies in the philosophy of clothes.*

Her clothes—green, yellow, diamond white,
lime and blue—hang in an enormous
French armoire. If you were to look
from through slips and silky dresses,
skirts, nylons, panties, maybe
a dress held to hide
black slacks and shoes,
you could see her hands
are there, finally, where, all along
your insides, typically sick with desire,
had wanted them.

4. *Your eye-glass is thicker than a Cuckold's horn.*

And now, sighing
softly, when she calls
you from the closet, from behind
the rustle of delicate clothes, the blur
of thick fish glass, the obscurity
of a mirror through a window,

I am there, with my own hands
buried deep

in a moon-black suit, hat,
tie, shoes, cufflinks and watch.
Even dark heavy glasses
slipping downward off my nose.
I push them back, delicately, and watch
the wardened perspective close.

The Etched Catastrophe

A Sunday night, the most predestined
        night of the week, ten o'clock,
           the etching *Ed Asleep*
falls against the table, where
              at the edge
           the plate of glass
              explodes, arcing
in tumultuous triumph
across the floor. The saltimbanque cat
        does an awesome twist
        as he scatters with the glass
      sliding out the door. A Brueghel freak,
        my wife slams into the room,
           straight from the shower, shouts
for a broom, and grimaces. She has
             a green towel around her head, tucked
           under like some post-medieval
        hood, a pink fringed robe
          with tattered beads, and silver
        chains that flash
with the broom as she slaps
against the glass. The shards
        collect themselves
          into a tower
of Babel. The cat, the sitter
          for this etched catastrophe, preens
         his head around the corner
and sleepwalks to the couch.
          Now on the wall is nothing but a nail.
      Tomorrow, everyone must suffer.
        Except for Ed, the cat,

who has been claimed by fame and art.
He, the climax of the week,
has no more pressing duty
than to sleep.

Longing

A rat emerges from the blue in the toilet beneath me
with a splash. His black eyes and tiny paws
swim around in circles
making but a small baby's paddling sound.
Next thing I know, he is up the narrow dark tunnel of my penis,
followed by rat after rat after rat.

When I am full—the kidneys, the heart, the blue spleen—
they fight, devour, have babies after babies
and fight some more for more room.

My head aches in middle age.
My skin bulges soft in places.
The rats' fat furry bellies press against the skin.

Dumbfounded, I fold the newspaper,
return to my wife waiting in our bed
and according to previous plans
proceed to try and make love.
Sensing a change in me, she grows cold, changing herself.
Slowly, to the dark familiar rhythm,
into my beady black eyes she climbs, joining love's friends.
I climb into her. And we are one.

Finished, I remove the sagging black prophylactic,
wet with rats, scratch for the pillow,
and turn to my side to sleep.
My wife sits up reading *National Geographic*
sadly stroking her tail, lonely and dissatisfied.
She wants desperately to see
if she too can have constant sex for seven days,

survive a fall from a five-story building,
walk away satisfied from a nuclear test,
somewhere in the oasis of a desert, the cool palm trees blowing
her shapely and young again.

For All Time

I saw my image in the match,
a black charred, curled figure
faced sideways in the ash.
The gray chunks rose up around me,
chiseled hatch marks, and their foam
collapsed with the fall of her finger
which flicked the tip
of the long cigarette. The other end
was red, and as it moved
to her lips, I saw myself
stretched out before her. The sun
was rouge and the fog rolled in
from nowhere. The ocean crashed
beneath this dark, but I could
only sense the motion. An old hat
was set beside me. Dragging
my legs, splotched with the sun,
the pant legs torn, I drew
my breath and climbed inside.
I was half memorized, fossilized
for future generations: a black
charred, curled figure faced
forward in the ash.

The Grand Union

Until this moment, the only thing living
was the moon. The bright vibrating lights
of the grocery store changed everything
and on the way through the aisles
I knew nothing, but the bliss
of the plastic wrappings, and the stained
glimmer of the linoleum, and the rubber
on the carriage when I knocked it
against the shelf. And on the way out

the cashier, in beautiful synthetic red,
cast back to tradition, offering me
a paper bag
without my asking, when I had so wanted
plastic, with its open frankness, showing everyone
what I had planned to eat.

"All right if I put everything in one bag?"
she asked with that knowing look.
And I said nothing but an assenting
nod, and so she added,
"I doubled it, so it should hold."
She carefully placed it in my arms.

The moon was gone, swallowed by the weather,
the parking lot lights
played host to a barrage of bugs, and my tires turned
somehow differently, as the trees,
with their artificial look, began to sway.

But the bag was still there, beside me
on the seat, double strength and brown. Paper,
with blurred green lettering that read
                    GRAND
                    UNION
and in the center of the letters (obliterating the A)
was a large red circle. Which meant what?
I will have to ask my wife
when I marry.

The Grand Canyon

I.

So I packed all my bags, drank a quick soda
of cacti, and headed out the door. I tripped
in a tiny hole
and fell face forward in the dirt.

The world spread out before me. The colors
ranged themselves in mixtures and in lines.
Reds mostly, but also tans, blues, greens,
some lemons and some limes.

Mules were descending steep paths.
People were hollering to hear their sound.
"Sweet meats! Sweet meats!" a man's voice swelled.
"Over here! Over here!"
the woman's voice, with its gentler, higher,

yet more cavernous tones.
Someone was snuffing my head: a desert rat
or one of those famous foxes, coyotes,
howling in silence at my nose.

II.

Someone told me they'd moved it.
Others that they'd covered it with sheets.
Someone else said it didn't even exist.

I stood at the window and watched
the sun through the burning haze.

I had on a black suit and thought
of calling you just to say
hello, but that word echoed
against my head until it died. A jet
tumbled over in the sky. The earth shook,
and a series of chasms slit the world.

Somewhere in North America,
there's a huge red hole. Somewhere,
north of here, there's beauty,
love, adventure. Whatever
that all means, all
it means. I turn about, south,
holding onto my half-deaf ears,
waiting for the jet, for the jet, for the jet

to pass, then all is silence
as the earth closes, the rumors true,
and the telephone sits steady in its sound.

III.

A lemon-lime tint accosts me, quivering a little,
as I rage to the outer edge
of the Grand Canyon. You've never been there,
and you say you'll never go. But here we are!
Me in my khakis; you in your blue skirt,
yellow faded top, wooden shoes.
You'll never wear that black dress I'd imagined,
and you'll never dye it red, or new.

The Ford's door is caved, the seat hot,
the clock slowed, suspended, completely worn out.
Sarcastic tints of lemon, or lime.
But nothing matters with all this stone.

Come on, get out of the car
before I strike you blind. I'd like to—
if only I could back it off
and fall right in.

The dust rises now
in little cups.
The sun spirals down
in gouges, made by rakes, dragged around
by mules, sweating into black, blinded
by the same. You brought the cards,
but no one's betting. There's not even room
for kissing, this land's so tough.

Hold my hat, while I hold you hard.
Lust is like a canyon—steep, rugged,
a long way down. Leave the car there,
the mules, the rope.
We'll stagger this land alone.
Neither one knows the way, but the distance
drags us to.
                    Two-thirty a.m.

The bottom, the starless height, a hot
dime in my one chest pocket. And that dark
sweat red
disfigures the only sky.

IV.

So, this is it,
the hole we've been begging for.
It's more than a fist,
but less than a soul.
More than I'd give in to.

We love it
and all its built-up majesty.
No, I've never been there
and I'll probably never go.

But something tells me
there'll be hell to pay.
And that the desert's
here at home.

· IV ·

A Small Cluster of Stars

A Small Cluster of Stars

I.

The Birds Fly Away

Cheap metal desk. My left shoe precariously set
on top of right, both balanced
on wheel-like spigot, a squeak, slow turning, the noisy iron
start of puddle, my bare fingers hurting, gripping
the cold chipped sill, chin barely reaching, scraping,
green folders, metal rods, an upward glance
to the clock, whips for hands, disappointment, the slowness, I watch

my father open the freezer and drop
a fist of crushed ice into his glass. The bourbon
browns the window; the oil-like alcohol
swirls downward, through the frost, and into the mud.

Two deep rows of four-drawer cabinets,
brown baked enamel, reinforced steel.
The open files, the closed files, the incomplete.
He adds a lemon, squeezing the rind, flicking
the burning bitter juices
off his ring-heavy hand, a possessed conductor
bringing down a Beethoven weight,

into the cage, at the canary. The black AT&Ts,
their magical ringing. The sharpener, the pencils,
the electrical grinding, the oppressive
itch of shaved wood.

Go into the fields or down the lane,
but don't go into Mr. McGregor's garden.
Your father had an accident there.
He was put in a pie.

The pale bird chirps frantically
and settles in a corner of its cage.
Then my mother comes back into view
yelling something
as she submerges her ringless long fingers
into the sink for another potato. I scratch
like a cat at the glass to scare her.
The lighted screens, their squat boxes. The threatening
tan keys. I open the door to the night
without knocking. The knife slides upward, scraping the bone.
One letter torn, two piles of mail, miscellaneous envelopes.

Babar is riding happily on his mother's back
when a wicked hunter, hidden behind some bushes,
shoots at them. The hunter has killed Babar's mother.
The monkey hides. The birds fly away. Babar cries.

II.
Dear Mother, Dear Father

Dear Mother:
I woke up troubled as your muffled moans
of pain rose through the floorboards and rolled

like smoke up along the walls.
What was hurting you, making you cry
in such an ugly, unmotherly way?
I climbed out of bed and placed
my left ear on the cold floor.
The smoke billowed upward; I couldn't hear a thing.
Then I started choking. I knew what it meant.
But why wasn't the smoke alarm blasting
its predestined warning to the world? My eyes burned
     and I felt like a fool. Then I started to cry.

    Detergents, ammonia, softeners and bleach.
    Through the cellar window I saw you
    on the floor, slumped by the dryer, buried in dry clothes,
    crying softly into your hands, the washer
    violently shaking, its last spin.
    Spray starch, stain remover, a dirty cotton mop.

Dear Father:
Mother was working and I couldn't find you.
Two, three hours and you still weren't home.
The car was there; I knew you couldn't be far.
Last time I knew you were watching t.v. while
I was in the basement building something out of wood.
Those people you talk of, from work, the ones who hate you,
I thought they'd come and stabbed you, dragged your body up the road.
Then Mr. McGregor told me you went into the Cooks'.
I saw you through the window. Mr. Turner was there,
and Charlie's mother. Fat Mrs. Cook

was snuggling on your lap, holding her glass
up against your chest. You were laughing
and everyone was drinking. I tripped
on Mr. McGregor's fence and slid
into our yard. A dose of chamomile tea,
one tablespoon to be taken at bedtime.

Acrylic latex paint, turpentine, plastic wood.
One summer afternoon I found you singing
drunkenly on the basement's bottom wooden step.
You laughed that no one loved you and if we loved you
it was not enough.
Grease and oil, steel wool, razor blades, gray permanent masking tape.

III.
On the Bottom Step

Down in the cellar, on the bottom step,
I gather together
myself in a tight knot, and look up
at the bulkhead door. Thin stripes of light
separate the old painted planks, and a bag of potatoes,
rotting, spills out across the rough cement. One small potato,
fist-sized, fallen furthest from the bag, displays dirty
white nubs. "I don't care what happens,
I'll not have another one of your mistakes. It's too painful."

A pile of books, mildewing, ruined. I pry

apart the pages. An ear ache.
My parents outside, their metal rakes scraping.

"That's disgusting to say that to the neighbors.
Why don't you invite them over and give a speech."
"I'll do it to the friggin neighbors if I want to; start with
old Mrs. Simpkins, lay her out right here on the lawn."
>The potato roots
>snap off easily
>with a flick
>of my thumb.
>Cheap metal desk.

Try to believe in the hope
of the clock. The black arrows,
they have to point somewhere.

Dear Mrs. Simpkins: We are pleased to enclose. Sincerely yours.
In lieu of the fact. We appreciate the opportunity to.
One of our very best products. Brass bent in the shape
of a huge paper clip, a Christmas gift, unique.
>The spine-cracked
>minutes. The minutely
>detailed hours. The striped
>light is blocked out with the groan of wood
>as they sit on the bulkhead door
>talking quietly now about the neighbors.

Then the neighbors fade,
a distant sea,

a shift in tone.

Then the wooden door rises.
And their voices, they lift up, rejoicing!
What is this empty place? A new kind of raking,
a hollow echoing, the burning claws
down the metal sheets, a thousand
times worse, on the inside of the skull.
I stop listening
and look down under the stairs. Furthest back, in the dust,
a screwdriver and a plastic toy.

Where out,
or into? The hard disks
chatter like rats.

IV.

A Small Black Box

I'm addicted to my job.
That's why they call me
Coo-Coo Bob.
I bob upon the sea all day.
But I never forget to collect my pay.

> We climbed down the bulkhead stairs, staring
> at my mother and your three brothers.
> She hung the damp wash, and they swung appealingly
> from the clothesline's metal rails.
> My father's tools lined the wall,

his equipment arranged
neatly on plywood shelves.
There were jars of screws, bolts and nails,
the clothes washer (no dryer then), and the broken mower
with the blade bent back, still clung
to the stench of old, wet grass.
Cellar smells: grained cement
and the stifling
seepage of earth and rain.

Vinyl-covered seats with metal frames.
This one swivels and the back adjusts.
A round glass table with magazines.
Fortune, Time, Field & Stream.
Yellow ruled pads, Rolodex files,
neat little rows,
the entire alphabet, nothing under Z.

You leaned against
the wooden step
and made me snuff
your crack and bum.
I wanted to, and did, until
you cried
and ordered me to stop.
All the while, I heard
my mother talking,
and your brothers laughing
and the cars

moving by
on the long
narrow road.

A new silence.
I hear the click behind me.
A boy of ten, I look into the frameless mirror
and see myself suddenly, reformed: a man, early forties,
surprisingly composed and becoming. Becoming?
Comely. I unbutton my top button
and still try to neaten my tie. Another door: a visitor.

Through a tunnel
the still-hot cinders drop
to the basement,
a small black box
with a small black door.

V.

The Inner House

I climb the larger set of stairs
to the inner house,
place my ear to the door, shut off my breath
and wait at the top, in darkness.
I hear the television from the den
and my brothers wrestling, fighting about stations.
I can tell from the voices no one else is home.

Black-framed, red-lighted Exit sign.

The lively click of the large metal door.
Be with you in just a moment.
Coffee? Rubber bands, the broken fax.

Then I hear a door and the bird from the kitchen.
I descend and return
to the bulkhead. I climb down under the stairs
and crawl in the dust to the back wall. Shuddering,
I begin to send out roots. Shuddering, I begin to send out roots.
It's easy to see roots three decades removed.
They snap off easily with a flick of my thumb.

Two dollars for certified. Twelve for express.
Handheld or automatic? The IN box,
the OUT box. Do you have the McGregor file? No.
And Babar's? Flick them with my thumb. A small cluster

of stars on the brown potato's
dusty underside. One childhood scar: the iron runner
of the large wooden sled
that fell against my face
when I tried to pull it down
by its rope
one summer several years ago.

My parents thought it was on purpose.
Because of their reproof,
I thought it was on purpose.
It was not on purpose. With the thumb.
I scratch it on my cheek.

VI.

In Silence

I scratch it on my cheek and rise
to get another file. The men arrive
in rubber boots and direct the cement
hose through the basement window.
I crouch beneath the stairs and watch
the embryonic weight approach.

After thirty years of waiting
in the underbrush, impatiently, his anger rising and falling
as steadily as his sword
at innocent branches that fell with ease, too simply
into silence, his guilt rising as easily,
he heard his enemies and he crouched
tensely until they came before him. And then he
lunged through the branches, out of hiding,
onto the pathway, roaring at the top of his lungs.
But it was only a peasant family
on their way to the village. They fell to the dirt
trembling.

But it was too late now to make mistakes.
He watched them fall
the way the branches fell.
And he wiped his blade. But a clean blade
is like silence—there is much guilt in silence—
and he climbed back into hiding
and continued his wait.
Through the secret opening, he carefully watched

the bodies lying on the path, their slow decay,
his slow recognition. Trembling, he cut
his cheek with the iron blade
and reveled in the trickle of blood.

I can hear the slow dripping
behind me, by the computer,
its chattering, the noisy iron,
start of puddle, slow turning,
a squeak, barely balancing,
the wheel-like spigot, the hot metal strokes.

VII.
Three Angels

Three angels on a tray
held outward in my hands,
I rise through the cellar door
into the kitchen.
Father holds a halo
over my head, and Mother
bears for me a candle
made of gold. Upward
in the overhead light
I see the yellow ring
and blinking somewhere
down below
a beautiful small
cluster of stars.

AUTHOR'S NOTES

Lines 23–26 of "A Small Cluster of Stars" from *The Tale of Peter Rabbit* by Beatrix Potter published by Frederic Warne and Company, N.Y., N.Y.

Lines 38–41 of "A Small Cluster of Stars" from *The Story of Babar, The Little Elephant* by Jean De Brunhoff, translated by Merle Haas, published by Random House, N.Y., N.Y.

The quotations opening each section of "Transmigrations of the Innocent" are from the following: 1. *Alba: The Month's Mind of a Melancholy Lover* by Robert Toft; 2. *The Rime of the Ancient Mariner* by Samuel Taylor Coleridge; 3. *Sartor Resartus* by Thomas Carlyle; and 4. *The Winter's Tale* by William Shakespeare.